The People in our Lives:
Everyday Psychology

The People in our Lives: Everyday Psychology

Dr Gagandeep Kaur

Highbrow Scribes Publications
New Delhi

Dedication

This book is dedicated to my parents.

Brigadier K.S. Mander: Papa, you went too soon.

Mrs Jaswinder Kaur: Mama, I miss you every single day. You taught me what love was.

I hope I make you proud.

Till we meet again.

Contents

Acknowledgements

Writing this book has been a journey of passion, dedication and unwavering support from many incredible individuals. First and foremost, I would like to extend my heartfelt gratitude to Jasmeet Walia, the brilliant founder of Fusion Lit. Jasmeet, your keen editorial insights and tireless efforts as my literary agent have been invaluable. Your guidance has not only refined my work but also elevated it to new heights. Thank you for believing in me and for your selfless support throughout this process.

A special thanks to Highbrow Scribes Publications and their phenomenal team. Your commitment to bringing this book to life, from the initial manuscript to the final publication, has been nothing short of extraordinary. Each of you has played a pivotal role in making this dream a reality, and for that, I am eternally grateful.

To my readers, thank you for embarking on this journey with me. Your support and enthusiasm are the driving forces behind every word written. I hope this book stirs your hearts and ignites your passions. And lastly, a big shout out to my family for supporting all my endeavours.

Happy reading!

About the Author

Dr Gagandeep Kaur is both a Doctor and a Health and Wellness Coach. Having completed her medical degree from Pune University and has over 20 years of experience in the medical field, Dr Gagandeep Kaur is passionate about the need for a more holistic approach towards treating a person rather than just giving medication for a particular disease.

This approach is what has led her to explore the various aspects of a person and has motivated her to write this book. She is on a constant endeavour to find ways to improve oneself and live a more meaningful life on earth hoping to make a positive change, however small, to the lives of people she has touched.

Introduction

Why did I write this book?

The answer lies in all the life I have lived so far.

The earliest memories I have are as an eight-year-old playing hide and seek with my friends in our house. A lot of memories persist after that....... randomly related to some events, a movie, a function, happy occasions, getting scolded, crying, feeling lost, unhappy, excited and a wide range of emotions. The most common thread in all these events are the people I can see and feel in those memories. As an only child of a mother who was socially a recluse, I did not learn much about people and how they behave till much later. It took me years to understand a person's intentions and I still make mistakes. After my parents passed, it took me time to find myself and realize that the bliss my mother felt in her solitude was what all of us are searching for eventually. Every person is unique, no two people will think alike. This is my attempt to make sense of this crazy world and to finally heal. I am hoping that by understanding how people work, I may see some understanding of the things they do and why. Though not an extensive study it is my first attempt to help myself and others.

CHAPTER 1

Life

The cycle of birth and life is Nature's phenomenon and as human beings, we are tied to this vicious cycle. The beauty of this life is that we do not know for how many years we shall live on this planet yet it is our hope and belief that keeps us going.

We spend the majority of our lives doing mundane chores to fulfil our basic needs like bathing, eating, sleeping, education, job, marriage, shopping, etc. Amidst these endeavours, we shall go through a new experience each day – happiness, sadness, perils, betrayal, mistakes, learnings, triumphs, etc. – not necessary in this order. Irrespective of the roles we play as a child, spouse, parent and professional, these experiences shall always remain a part of our lives.

Gradually, as we progress in life, we gain intellect and wisdom and we realise that in the end, only one thing matters the most in life – relationships.

No matter whether you own an expensive car, a sprawling mansion and a seven-figure bank balance, if you have no one to share your endeavours, your life is fruitless.

Happiness is the core element to a healthy living. Sadness and loneliness are our foes. So how can we make our journey worth living? It is through living the moment, acknowledging different experiences and acquiring new learnings. Is this possible without having people around you and engineering a relationship? You already know the answer.

As a medical student, I was constantly studying the human body and mind. A patient will share the symptoms. However, there are signs that as a doctor, I can see without a patient sharing with me their physical or mental ailments. By examining a patient's mind and body, I can diagnose the root cause of the problem.

I feel that in practical life too we consciously or unknowingly perceive others based on our knowledge and understanding. People communicate by sharing stories, gossip, personal experiences, memories, etc. With patience and an unbiased mind, you must learn to observe and understand the other person's point of view. This will not only help you to come to a better conclusion but also strengthen your bond with them. Such an experience will become a blessing.

Every situation has consequences which depend upon your reaction. Greeting someone in the room with a smile irrespective of whether the person is good or bad, makes a big difference in your life. You earn compassion no matter if the other person does not reciprocate.

I am not dictating to you to follow any thumb

rule. I want you to be in complete control of your situation rather than being controlled.

I started this book by talking about the vicious cycle of birth and death. Most of you may not agree with me but I strongly believe in this theory that we all have a soul and our body is the medium to go through the cycle of life and death.

I consider a soul to be an energy belonging to a higher realm. We are sent in our mortal bodies to learn and elevate ourselves to the ultimate level where we will then merge with our source and will no longer need to come back as a human being. In simple terms – to fulfil our karmic cycle. No matter which religion we follow, our scriptures and holy texts always talk of a higher energy guiding us.

We may define our rebirth as a reincarnation of the soul and our death as going back to our Maker. In each cycle of birth and death, there is a new opportunity to learn how to live our lives better in that particular epoch.

Talking about divine energy may seem a dichotomy to science which was my subject when I was striving to become a doctor. However, I believe that there are certain realms which are beyond the reach of science and can only be comprehended through experiences.

I envision the body as a medium to travel through the time I am on earth. As mortal beings, we are mostly obsessed with worldly possessions – money, luxury, comfort, status – and we remain entangled in this maze. And when we reflect upon our life lived so far, we realise that we have never utilised our time efficiently and now our end is near. Many such books have been written on the ethics of living.

We have discussed how to elevate our karma, the energy we accumulate throughout our lives. Over the centuries, the human condition has been studied from many perspectives. Medical sciences have examined the ailments of the body and mind, seeking ways to cure illnesses. Astronomy has endeavoured to study the planets and the moon, seeking answers to why certain phenomena occur. Psychology aims to understand and explain behaviours. Human beings are capable of performing acts of great kindness as well as committing horrific deeds against each other and themselves.

What prompts us to take certain actions? Where do we come from? Where do we go ultimately? No one has a precise answer because we cannot interact with those who have left for their heavenly abode.

We live our lives with hope and belief. Our culture teaches us that our life is karma which is divided into good and bad. If we lead an honest and spiritual life, we shall find a place in heaven. Those who are dishonest and commit sins shall rot in hell.

To me, all life leads to this hope: the hope that I can become a better version of myself through learning and the hope that I can make my life worthy of my time here on Earth.

CHAPTER 2

Who am I?

Who am I? This is the simplest question with a complex answer. Can we truly define our identity? If you respond that I am a child, parent, spouse, sibling, professional, etc., these all are the different roles that we play in our everyday lives.

Then how can we define ourselves? By understanding our purpose in life, working on our mission and fulfilling our responsibilities in society. Can we accomplish them without supporting one another? Definitely not.

Life is all about meeting people from different walks of life while we are treading on our path to achieve our goals. Some will become our lifetime companions. Some will act as our advisors and teach us a lesson. While some will meet us only once. These relationships will determine the quality of our life.

A single mistake is enough to ruin your relationship and cause eternal heartbreak. Does it mean that this will happen one day or the other? Absolutely not!

As I have said in the beginning, once we understand ourselves, we will learn to empathise with others. This will not only help us to handle everyday situations but will also help us to understand ourselves much better.

Now if I ask you who are you? Your answer could be – I am a body, a soul or a person There is no precise definition to describe anyone,

The dictionary defines a person as a human being regarded as an individual.

It might sound vague but that is how the theory goes. A person is said to have both physical (tangible) and intangible existence. Our body and sense organs help to define our physical form while our mind is without any form and it can only be felt through awareness and experience.

What about consciousness and soul? It depends upon our beliefs. They are not visible yet they are a part of our being.

It is also true that more than the physical presence it is always the nonphysical mind that will play the biggest role in a person's life.

Combining both our body and mind, there is one organ that determines our every move and action – Our Brain.

A brain is defined as the organ within the skull that controls movements, thoughts, memories and feelings.

Then what is the role of the mind? The mind is the mechanism that signals the brain to perceive, think, feel and react.

The brain is treated by neurosurgeons and neuro physicians while the mind is studied and treated by a psychiatrist or a psychologist. The major difference between the two is that the brain has a physical presence. It can be seen, touched and operated upon. It has different parts like the cerebellum, cerebrum and brain stem. The cerebrum is the part of the brain which is responsible for our sensory, motor and higher functions. Damage to the brain can result in a marked change in the quality of life one leads. This is why the physical well-being of the brain is paramount.

The mind on the other hand can only be studied through a person's thoughts, reactions and memory. There is no physical presence of any of these yet they exist. A change in the quality of a person's mind can also have far-reaching consequences on their own well-being as well as their life with others. The mind thus is equally important.

Mind is defined as that part of a person that thinks, Imagines, remembers and takes action. It is what makes a person capable of doing things in the world.

Psychologists have classified the mind into the conscious and the subconscious mind. The conscious mind creates awareness and the ability to think and remember. The subconscious mind may not always be actively used. It comprises our perceptions, thoughts, expectations and biassed behaviour. These attributes are what make a person.

Each person holds distinct attributes based on the various factors in their lives. This is what makes life interesting. You can never predict what a person will say or do when faced with a certain situation. Sometimes you may not even be able to predict your reactions.

We often talk about the longevity of our life. Death is inevitable and unpredictable yet we still wonder about our life span.

A life span can be defined as the time between birth and death. The average life expectancy over the years has gradually risen between seventy and seventy-five years. This is because of a number of reasons like safer environments, improved medical resources, better nutrition and many other factors. In the early centuries, the issues were always about survival against the environment or disease; this has gradually changed. Most of us will live a life close to our life expectancy unless killed in an accident, natural disaster or due to a fatal medical condition. The challenge now has come to be about how to have a better quality of life. This extends to most areas of our day-to-day living. We want to have a higher standard of living, eat healthy food, have better health and also happy relationships. We constantly strive for this. We educate ourselves, we get jobs or start a business, we meditate, we exercise and perform lots of other activities. We work to make ourselves and others better.

As human beings, we need to understand that each of our lives is but a journey. An individual journey towards a higher and better self. We cannot be more than a witness to each other's lives.

Parents are a means for the soul to reincarnate onto this earth and live its life span.

A sibling is a companion who from their birth is joined to us by karmic bonds that have resulted in us having the same set of parents.

A spouse is but a witness to our journey and an energy being who will help to bring more souls into this life, connected to us through old connections.

In the end, each of us is alone. Why did I say this?

We may support each other, we may help each other and be there for each other but the suffering whether physical or mental is yours alone. No matter how close you are, you cannot feel their physical pain. You can hold their hand and comfort them but that is as far as you can go. The sooner we understand this the easier and better it is for us.

Since time immemorial, humans have been interested in studying other humans. How does the body and mind work? What causes disease? Why do some people get sick and die earlier while others live a long life? These are some of the questions that have been raised over many decades. Interest in the human mind and body has been documented in ancient civilizations. Cultures throughout history have given birth to many inquisitive minds who made attempts to answer these questions. This led to the development of the various branches of science.

For example, the study of life is called biology.

Biology is thus defined as the study of living organisms, divided into many specialised fields that cover their morphology, physiology, anatomy, behaviour, origin and distribution. Aristotle is regarded as the Father of Biology.

Sociology is the study of human life and culture.

Why do we want to study life?

To better understand ourselves and those around us and to live our lives in a good and productive manner as opposed to just passing our time on earth before we die.

It is personally important for me to know that I didn't just go through life without making any contribution to myself, my family and society. No matter how small my contribution may be, I must have the satisfaction of knowing I did my best.

Within the framework of my life, encompassing both the parameters that were predetermined and those I set for myself, I did my best.

Life doesn't just happen to us; it simply happens.

Each day, the sun will rise and set and because we are alive on this planet, we will experience this, along with the changing weather and seasons specific to our region.

All of this will happen and is beyond my control, as well as anyone else's. However, many things are within my control. Life may be happening constantly, but it is happening to me. My singular life is mine alone. No one else is living these particular days that are mine to experience. My set of circumstances – my parents, my children, my work – are all unique to me. If I choose to, I can control and change many things in this life.

CHAPTER 3

Stages of Life

We now know that our life is a cycle of birth and death. Anything that exists on earth is mortal and will perish at different periods.

In one lifetime, we go through different stages. The process starts with copulation which is the source of creation. This human creation goes through various phases as they progress with age and time. This process is inevitable. The difference lies in how you make efficient use of the years you live by with your karma.

Erik Erikson, a famous 20th century German psychologist believed that life could be divided into eight stages known as the **8 Stages of Development Theory.**

These stages were:

1. Infancy

2. Early Childhood

3. Preschool

4. School Age

5. Adolescence

6. Young Adulthood

7. Middle Adulthood

8. Late Adulthood

Each stage shapes our life in terms of growth and development. Different stages in our lives have different needs. Relationships will change. What seemed extremely relevant at a young age will no longer be of much concern a few years down the line.

At each stage, individuals face and ideally master new challenges, which Erikson called psychosocial crises. Successful resolution of these crises leads to the development of a healthy personality and the acquisition of basic virtues. Here are the stages:

Infancy (0-1 year) - Trust vs. Mistrust:

Babies are magical creatures. A woman transforms into a mother when her baby is born, marking the beginning of a new chapter in her life. Babies bring hope for the future. They develop new relationships with us and we step into new roles as siblings, grandparents, aunts, uncles, etc.

A baby lives its life on instincts and reflexes, unaware of the past, present and future. Their life is unplanned and they live entirely in the moment.

John Bowlby was the first psychologist who studied children and their relationships with the people around them. He worked on what effects separation had on babies and also how they formed bonds and attachments.

It was believed that a baby was mainly attached

to the person who took care of their nourishment and needs. So by default, they were attached to the mother as she fed the baby and provided physical comfort and safety.

A mother is a primary caregiver who proactively responds to her child's needs. This was not only seen as a learned behaviour but also as an evolutionary one. In tough circumstances, babies who had someone to look after them were more likely to survive than those who did not receive proper care.

In the 1970s, Mary Ainsworth, a psychologist, expanded on John Bowlby's work and conducted the remarkable **Strange Situation Study.**

The study aimed to observe how infants respond to separation and reunion with their mothers, thereby identifying different patterns of attachment. Here is a detailed description of the experiment:

The Experiment Design

The Strange Situation procedure involves a series of eight episodes, each lasting about three minutes, designed to progressively increase the stress experienced by the infant. The study is typically conducted in a lab setting equipped with a one-way mirror for unobtrusive observation.

Procedure

1. Introduction (Episode 1):

Participants: The mother (or primary caregiver), the infant (aged 12-18 months) and a stranger.

Setting: A room with toys to create a comfortable environment for the child.

Action: The mother and the infant enter the room and the child is allowed to explore.

2. Mother and Infant Alone (Episode 2):

Action: The mother sits quietly while the infant is free to explore the room and the toys.

3. Stranger Enters (Episode 3):

Action: A stranger enters the room, talks with the mother and then approaches the infant to engage in play. The mother is still present.

4. Mother Leaves, Stranger Stays (Episode 4):

Action: The mother exits the room, leaving the infant with the stranger. The stranger attempts to comfort and play with the infant if they become distressed.

5. Mother Returns, Stranger Leaves (Episode 5):

Action: The mother returns to the room and the stranger leaves. The mother comforts the infant if needed and then encourages them to explore again.

6. Mother Leaves, Infant Alone (Episode 6):

Action: The mother leaves the room again; this time leaving the infant alone.

7. Stranger Returns (Episode 7):

Action: The stranger re-enters the room and

tries to comfort and engage the infant.

8. Mother Returns (Episode 8):

Action: The mother returns and the stranger leaves. The mother comforts the infant if necessary and allows them to explore once more.

Observations and Attachment Styles

Throughout these episodes, observers record the infant's behaviour, focusing on key aspects such as:

Exploration: The infant's willingness to explore the room and play with toys, both in the presence of the mother and the stranger.

Reaction to Separation: The infant's response when the mother leaves the room.

Reaction to Reunion: The infant's behaviour when the mother returns.

Based on these observations, Ainsworth identified three primary attachment styles:

1. Secure Attachment:

Behaviour: Infants feel confident to explore when their mother is present, show distress when she leaves and are quickly comforted upon her return.

Implication: Indicates a healthy attachment and a sense of security in the caregiver's presence.

2. Insecure-Avoidant Attachment:

Behaviour: Infants show little emotional

response when the mother leaves and avoid her upon return. They may not explore much, preferring to stay close to the caregiver or toys without interacting.

Implication: Suggests an underlying sense of insecurity, potentially due to a caregiver's rejection or unavailability.

3. Insecure-Resistant (or Ambivalent Attachment):

Behaviour: Infants are highly distressed when the mother leaves and are not easily comforted upon her return. They may seek contact but also resist it, displaying ambivalence.

Implication: Indicates anxiety and insecurity, possibly stemming from inconsistent caregiver responsiveness.

Ainsworth's research has had a profound impact on understanding early childhood development and the importance of caregiver-infant attachment in shaping future emotional and social behaviour.

The infancy stage can be summed up as follows:

Crisis: Infants must learn to trust their caregivers to meet their needs.

Successful Resolution: If caregivers provide reliable care and affection, the child develops a sense of trust.

Virtue: Hope.

Early Childhood (1-3 years) - Autonomy vs. Shame and Doubt:

In this stage, the child now begins to explore his surroundings. This is also where many milestones will be achieved like crawling, walking and talking. He understands the difference between praise and discouragement. The toddler years are a time of emotional, social and cognitive development. Along with physical development like fine and gross motor skills, vision and hearing, the child also develops social skills. A toddler learns that they are a separate being from their mother. They may be able to recognize themselves in the mirror. A toddler also throws a lot of tantrums; this is mainly because of their frustration at not being able to communicate what their needs are unlike older children.

Parents who are emotionally stable themselves are better able to handle this phase in the child and their life. This can be a challenging time for both.

Some small things can go a long way in helping. For example:

1. Setting up a routine. Routine gives comfort and stability to the day.

2. Playing in a proper place for a fixed amount of time can have soothing effects on the toddler.

3. Playing a similar musical record so that the child recognizes it will also help.

4. Have well-established yes and no patterns. This will help in avoiding confusion for the

child. If you say no to a particular thing today do not allow it the next day.

5. Allow the child freedom to explore.

Constantly discouraging the child or always saying no to everything will result in a fearful child with low confidence.

Crisis: As toddlers begin to assert their independence, they must learn to do things for themselves.

Successful Resolution: If caregivers encourage self-sufficient behaviour, children develop a sense of autonomy. Over-criticism or control can lead to feelings of shame and doubt.

Virtue: Will.

Preschool (3-6 years) - Initiative vs. Guilt:

Children of this age are just learning to be independent and do things for themselves. This is also the time when you will start noticing a distinct nature of the child emerging.

Crisis: Children need to begin asserting control and power over their environment.

Successful Resolution: If children are allowed to initiate activities and interact with others, they develop a sense of initiative. If not, they may feel guilty about their needs and desires.

Virtue: Purpose.

School Age (6-12 years) - Industry vs. Inferiority:

This is the time in most countries when school starts. Children learn to interact with their own age group. The concept of friend and teacher is introduced. The child now has the ability to stay away from home for a fixed period of time knowing and realising that they can come back to the known environment. Children will develop more self-awareness. They start to understand the people around them. Children also start to feel superior or inferior to their peers. They also start listening to what others are saying to them and about them.

These are crucial years for shaping a child's self-narrative. Parents need to be mindful of this as the things we repeatedly say to or about our children often become their reality over time.

Instead of saying, 'She is not good at maths,' you could say, 'She needs some extra help in maths' or 'She needs to work more on her maths skills.' We don't need to accept a lot of things as given; they can often be turned around. The children raised by a strong mother or caregiver who is willing to fight for them will be more successful in life, though this may sometimes lead to conflicts with them.

In a world of phones, iPads and 24/7 TV, child-rearing has sometimes become a battle. With more opportunities come more dangers that we need to protect them from. Speak to your child every day. Tell them you love them and that they can share anything and everything with you.

Crisis: Children need to cope with new social and academic demands.

Successful Resolution: Encouragement and praise for accomplishments lead to a sense of industry and competence, while failure or lack of encouragement can result in feelings of inferiority.

Virtue: Competence.

Adolescence (12-18 years) - Identity vs. Role Confusion:

This is the age of the hormonal changes that the human body goes through. It starts at 12 years and lasts up to 18 years of age. Children start to discover who they are. They are also going through immense physical and mental changes that are both confusing and exciting at the same time. It is not easy being a young person in today's society. Given the extent to which social media has taken over our lives, it is nearly impossible not to succumb to its lure. Boys and girls are equally susceptible. This can be an extremely challenging age. On one hand, children are dealing with significant physical development, including changes in body shape and size. On the other hand, these are crucial years when they are constantly reminded to focus on the future, study, pursue a career and live up to various expectations.

Crisis: Teens must develop a sense of self and personal identity.

Successful Resolution: The successful exploration of different roles and ideas leads to a strong sense of identity while failure to establish a clear identity results in role confusion.

Virtue: Fidelity.

Young Adulthood (18-40 years) - Intimacy vs. Isolation:

I call this the hard-working years. This is the time when we study in college (if we are lucky), get a job, build a career and build relationships. It is the time of competition, love, sex, bearing children and seeing your parents grow old. It can also be a time of immense emotional and spiritual growth. By this age, the majority of us will have developed some skills to understand the people around us. If not, we should work on developing these skills.

Every person you meet in your day-to-day life, including close family, will react or respond to you based on their own perception of the situation. Learning to understand their natures and reactions can help us manage daily stressors better and foster healthier relationships.

We also need to understand ourselves better. What is the point of understanding others if I cannot read myself clearly?

Crisis: Young adults need to form intimate, loving relationships with other people.

Successful Resolution: The successful relationships lead to feelings of intimacy and commitment while failure can result in loneliness and isolation.

Virtue: Love.

Middle Adulthood (40-65 years) - Generativity vs. Stagnation:

After many years of working, you might be nearing retirement or already retired. Your children may have grown up and settled down and you might be stable in your life. Depending on the preceding years, this can be a time of great happiness or unhappiness. Some people might look back and feel they wasted time or didn't achieve as much as they could have, possibly feeling bitter about perceived injustices.

This could also be the time when you plan for your old age. As we grow older, we become more set in our ways and inflexible about certain things. We have a clear idea of what we want and don't want. Making new friends can be difficult. Blessed are those who have friends they have grown older with, such as school and college friends. Numerous studies have shown that having friends in our older years plays a crucial role in maintaining a good quality of life as important as a good diet and regular exercise.

The first responsibility of parents lies with themselves. As we grow older and find ourselves with more free time, it becomes important to find ways to occupy and keep ourselves engaged.

Crisis: Adults need to create or nurture things that will outlast them, often by parenting children or contributing to positive changes that benefit others.

Successful Resolution: Feeling useful and accomplished leads to a sense of generativity while failure results in shallow involvement in the world.

Virtue: Care.

Late Adulthood (65+ years) - Integrity vs. Despair:

I once met a person in his 80s who was extremely disillusioned and unhappy. From my perspective, he should have been happy: he had a good career, was financially stable, in good health and all his children were well-settled. His children also took care of him but he remained unhappy. Every time I met him, he complained about many things – general issues, health concerns, other people and his children. Each time I came away feeling depressed.

This led me to question what his expectations were from life at this age. Why this unhappiness? The answer must be related to his past. Happiness is not something that other people can give him. It is something that will come from within.

Often, when a younger person meets someone from the geriatric age group, all they see is an old person. We rarely take a moment to reflect that this individual was once a child, a younger person, a bright newlywed or a new parent. A highly intelligent and evolved person might do this but most of us don't make the effort.

Old age brings many things. There are happy moments when you can look back and feel proud of your achievements and there are unhappy health issues. However, one thing that should never come with old age is a loss of dignity and self-respect.

Crisis: Older adults need to look back on life and feel a sense of fulfilment.

Successful Resolution: A sense of integrity and satisfaction from a life well-lived leads to feelings of wisdom while regret and dissatisfaction result in despair.

Virtue: Wisdom.

A life well lived should also have an equally dignified death.

Death is inevitable. It will happen to all of us. If a long, happy life has been lived then death should be seen as a joyous event – a passage from one lifetime on this earth with a certain set of souls, filled with love, until it is time to return to our Maker. However, this rarely happens. We fear death because we do not know what comes after.

No one who has died has come back to tell us about the afterlife. There are many accounts of life after death but what if those are just figments of someone's imagination? That said, no one has ever seen God either yet we all believe in a higher power. We love Him and pray to Him.

So, in our last moments, we must surrender and trust that He will take us home. We must believe that there is a home waiting for us when we leave this world.

Though rare, we must talk about our last moments with our loved ones. What do I want? Do I want to be admitted to the ICU and put on a ventilator when there might be little chance of recovery? As a doctor, I have encountered very few people who discuss this. It is considered inauspicious in most households. Children and parents rarely talk about death or hospitalisation. We prefer to wear blinders and pretend it will never happen. This is sad.

This is very important, yet people rarely address their own mortality. We all know we have to go but we don't want to talk about it. Why shouldn't I be able to decide my exit from this world with honour? We do not choose the moment of our birth, nor will we choose the moment of our death, but we can have a conversation about how far we want to go with all the treatments and resuscitation methods available to us.

This might be an easier topic for me as a medical professional, but it should be a conversation all parents have with their children, without it being a burden. Just as we prepare for a big event in our lives, we can prepare ourselves and our loved ones for this too.

In the twilight years, you don't need many people around you. You need just one person who stands by you and says, 'No matter what happens, I am here for you because I love you and care for you. I will make sure you are okay as long as you are with us. I will be unhappy when you go, but I want this time to be secure and safe for you. You don't need to feel scared because I am here.' That is all that is needed. One Person.

If I have that one person in my last days, I am blessed and I have truly lived a worthwhile life. This is love with pure intention – having someone care for you in your last moments simply because they love you.

CHAPTER 4

Identifying the Different Personalities

Personality is defined in the Oxford Dictionary as the combination of characteristics or qualities that form an individual's distinctive character.

Personality includes our patterns of thoughts, actions and emotions. It is also influenced by our environment.

Personality traits are characteristic patterns in how a person thinks and feels. For example, a person may be an introvert, arrogant, loyal, rude, nice, etc. These are some of the adjectives we commonly use to describe people.

Personality is not something we are born with. Instead, it is a combination of multiple factors:

- Genes
- Parenting style
- Early relationships
- Physical attributes
- Education
- Experiences

A person's personality may also change over time due to personal experiences, adverse events or age.

An extremely confident person may become unsure and show a lack of confidence after a business loss or a failed relationship. Similarly, a timid person may transform into a successful and outgoing person as they grow in life.

The goal of studying our own personality as well as that of others is to improve our quality of life by bringing about a change in ourselves.

Personality is one of the most studied aspects of psychology. Many studies have been conducted on personality over the ages, leading to the development of various methods and tests to classify different personality types.

Historically, Hippocrates described four personality types based on a person's temperament, which were believed to be linked to the predominant type of body fluid in the person's body.

The four types of temperaments based on body fluids were:

1. Blood: Sanguine

2. Phlegm: Phlegmatic

3. Yellow bile: Choleric

4. Black bile: Melancholic

While a person is never defined by a single quality, their overall personality often exhibits certain traits that can be categorised under a specific type. For example, people with a Sanguine personality were sociable, outgoing and optimistic. They were also easily bored and continuously sought out pleasure-seeking behaviour. They were easily distracted and needed entertainment.

The Choleric-type personalities were people with leadership qualities. They were confident, motivating and extroverts but could also be aggressive and dominating in nature.

A Phlegmatic person was found to have a quiet and calm disposition. They were kind, consistent and shy but could also be indecisive and low in confidence.

The Melancholic person was moody, cautious and pessimistic but could also be very loyal and a great planner and organiser.

Another way of classifying human beings was developed by William Sheldon based on a person's body structure. He thus classified people as:

1. Endomorphs

2. Ectomorphs

3. Mesomorphs

The following characteristics were attributed to each category:

1. **Endomorphs:** These were people who were jovial in nature with easygoing personalities. They were often overweight as they loved to

eat. The body type of such people was often round and short.

2. **Ectomorphs:** These people were described as tall but thin. They were supposedly physically weak but were also found to be mentally strong with calm composure and good intelligence.

3. **Mesomorphs:** These were the natural athletes with strong muscular bodies and a strong competitive spirit.

One of the recent classifications of personalities is based on the Myers-Briggs Model. Here the personality is divided into two main groups – the introverts and the extroverts. These were further classified based on various traits such as introversion, intuition, feeling and judgement.

Every human being is never just one colour but identifying a prominent personality trait can often make life easier for the person and those around them. In many cultures, arranged marriages often involve matching horoscopes, which historically served as a way to match personalities as well.

The zodiac also divides the calendar into twelve signs based on each sign's predominant traits. Here are the twelve zodiac signs along with their commonly associated personality traits:

1. **Aries (March 21-April 19):** Energetic, adventurous, dynamic and confident. Aries individuals are known for their leadership qualities and enthusiasm. They can also be impulsive and impatient.

2. **Taurus (April 20-May 20):** Reliable, patient, practical and devoted. Taurus individuals are known for their strong will and determination. They can also be stubborn and possessive.

3. **Gemini (May 21-June 20):** Adaptable, outgoing, intelligent and curious. Geminis are known for their versatility and communication skills. They can also be indecisive and inconsistent.

4. **Cancer (June 21-July 22):** Emotional, nurturing, intuitive and protective. Cancer individuals are known for their loyalty and empathy. They can also be moody and overly sensitive.

5. **Leo (July 23-August 22):** Confident, ambitious, generous and charismatic. Leos are known for their leadership and creativity. They can also be arrogant and stubborn.

6. **Virgo (August 23-September 22):** Analytical, practical, diligent and reliable. Virgos are known for their attention to detail and organisational skills. They can also be critical and overly cautious.

7. **Libra (September 23-October 22):** Diplomatic, charming, social and fair-minded. Libras are known for their sense of balance and justice. They can also be indecisive and avoid confrontations.

8. **Scorpio (October 23-November 21):** Passionate, resourceful, determined and

intuitive. Scorpios are known for their intensity and depth. They can also be secretive and jealous.

9. **Sagittarius (November 22-December 21):** Optimistic, adventurous, independent and philosophical. Sagittarians are known for their love of freedom and exploration. They can also be careless and tactless.

10. **Capricorn (December 22-January 19):** Disciplined, responsible, ambitious and practical. Capricorns are known for their strong work ethic and perseverance. They can also be pessimistic and reserved.

11. **Aquarius (January 20-February 18):** Innovative, independent, humanitarian and intellectual. Aquarians are known for their progressive thinking and originality. They can also be aloof and unpredictable.

12. **Pisces (February 19-March 20):** Compassionate, artistic, intuitive and gentle. Pisces individuals are known for their empathy and creativity. They can also be escapist and overly idealistic.

There are many personality tests that we can take or administer to others to gain a better understanding of them. It has been noted time and again that knowing and having better self-awareness is key to greater overall life satisfaction.

Why do we need to do all these classifications? Society often likes to group people into many categories. Certain traits may be seen more commonly in certain groups of people. For example, North Indians are seen as more jovial and outgoing, people from Bengal are more academic oriented, while in the south teaching children classical dance is a must. Different regions evolve different traits in the people living there.

There is a strong bias towards boys in all Asian countries, where the groom's family often expects gifts from the girl's family simply because they are from the groom's side.

We may believe that society has changed and we have all become more educated, but this is a myth. The only thing that has changed is that people now better hide what they actually think, or they pretend on social media platforms by posting happy pictures and glossing over the real issues.

This is concerning because it perpetuates false expectations. For instance, a daughter raised as an equal to her brother may not realise that after marriage, she is still expected to be the primary cook at home. Despite earning an equal salary to her spouse, she may face occasional judgement based on her cooking abilities. There may be a cook, but the primary responsibility of managing the day-to-day menu and food items often falls on her. Has anyone prepared the girl child for a future where, after having children, she will need to return to work and still manage the household and childcare?

Boys have it no better. In the past, they were often expected to earn money and that was enough;

girls respected them and listened to them. Along the way, we changed the rules without much explanation, leaving boys confused about their roles and expectations.

Nowadays, boys are expected to be macho but not overly so, earn more than their wives and still share equal responsibilities at home. We've changed the rules without fully letting go of many stereotypes. This has led to a lot of conflict within the society and confused individuals. This has also given rise to a person feeling more overwhelmed and anxious.This can be seen by the pressure young adults feel about their lives.There is a constant feeling of not being enough as you are. There is competition to do bigger better in almost everything, setting unrealistic standards for an individual. This needs to be toned down because it is a very unhealthy way to live. It puts a strain on the person as well as the family and all relationships suffer because of this.

Relationships

As we grow older and progress into adulthood, one key aspect of our lives is our relationships. It has been documented that people with happier relationships live longer and better lives. Therefore, the quality of your relationships significantly determines the quality of your life.

Relationships can be classified into those we are born with and those we create throughout our lives. Parents, siblings, children and relatives are our blood relations. These we can neither choose nor change.

Spouses, friends and colleagues are relationships over which we have some choice, though not entirely. For example, when I take up a new job, I do not choose my coworkers, but if I am excessively unhappy, I can change my job. All relationships in our lives influence us and vice versa. Some play important roles in shaping who we are as people.

Parents

The parents we are born to, the type of house and upbringing they provide, our siblings and our role in the family dynamics are life-altering factors that play major roles in shaping who we are as individuals. These factors are also rarely within our control.

Behind each relationship and every action within that relationship, there is always an intention. Our parents intend to raise good, self-sufficient children who make them proud. No parent ever wants to see a child suffer or fail. Within the parameters of their own lives, they try to do the best they can.

Our relationship with our parents will never remain the same. As children, we see them as everything in our lives. As teenagers, we may view them as slightly out of touch because we think we know better and their advice may sound dumb. Maturity is when we can see our parents with empathy, recognizing their own failings, dreams and thoughts. We must understand them without judgement. This phase often begins in our twenties, when we are somewhat grown up and maybe become parents ourselves.

This may also be the time when we recognize the negative traits in our parents' personalities. A parent who is self-obsessed, controlling, has anger issues, or refuses to allow you to make decisions can have long-lasting repercussions on your life. Recognizing our parents' personalities is just the beginning. We may never be able to change them but we can empower ourselves to handle these situations better. The reasons for their behaviour may be many and deeply rooted, often stemming from how they were brought up. While we cannot change their past, we can heal ourselves and help them heal as well by choosing not to judge but to accept with love.

In a few years, the roles will be reversed. Our parents will grow old and frail and we will become their caretakers. Few of us can understand and accept this transition well. How often can we listen to the same story about our childhood without asking them to stop? I would say many times. One day, there will be no one to tell those stories. One of the biggest losses I felt after both my parents passed away was that no one called me by my nickname anymore. No one knew my childhood stories. It took me many years to recover and heal but I still cannot say that I am completely fine. Some losses remain a wound throughout our lives.

As a child, one of the most difficult things to accept is the loss of a parent. No matter how prepared we are, it still hurts. The evolved among us may see this as a transition to the next phase in life, a return to our Maker but even spiritually sound people often struggle to cope. Accepting and understanding this loss as a part of life is one of the most difficult things you will ever do.

Siblings

Born to the same parents, siblings share the unique charm of knowing us from birth. It will also be the longest relationship you will ever have with anyone. Siblings, regardless of gender, can play a vital role in our lives. A good relationship with them can be the biggest support you need. Competition learned at home can prepare us for life outside. We often share a love-hate relationship with our brothers and sisters.

'I love you but I also feel like killing you at the same time.' How often have we felt this way? Well-developed and maintained sibling relationships can play a crucial role in adulthood, providing us with a strong sense of security. Like all relationships, this one also needs commitment and doesn't happen automatically.

Spouse/Partner

Love, as a noun, is defined as an intense feeling of deep affection. This is the foundation of one of the most beautiful relationships in our lives. The excitement and joy of crushes in school and college, the anticipation of meeting someone we may see as a future long-term partner, the process of getting to know each other and perhaps growing old together. In many cultures, arranged marriages are common. The people involved may not instantly fall in love but may agree to marry based on mutual respect and other obligations. Love may develop later on, not as an all-encompassing, passionate fire but as a slow burn. This relationship requires a lot of hard work, especially since it can be broken at any time. It is a legal arrangement and can therefore be undone easily too.

Children

To look upon a tiny human being and instantly love them is the essence of parenting. The human race does not need any qualifications to become parents, just biology. Most of us will experience a planned or unplanned pregnancy but we will still love our child no matter what. Children bring hope – the hope that everything we do in this lifetime is worthy.

There are many parenting styles and we never follow any style on purpose. Most often we react and try to do the best we can.

The conscious parenting involves letting go of our own desires and focusing on making the child a better, self-reliant human being. It requires a lot of self-awareness on the part of the parents, being acutely conscious of their own biases, emotions and expectations and not letting these cloud the child's perception of the world.

Often, the voice in our child's head will be our voice. The narrative we set for them must be always positive and encouraging. No one wants to raise unhappy children – that is never a parent's goal. However, constant expectations, whether expressed or implied, can have very negative, long-lasting effects on a child's life. There are many books available on raising better and more successful children. I have read a few and realised they all share a lot of common advice. Here are some key points I have picked up and thought would be useful to share:

1. Healing your own childhood as a parent

As a parent, it is important not to carry the burden of your own childhood into your parenting. As adults, we can try to heal our own hurts rather than passing them on.

2. Love and pure intention in parenting

Love and pure intention are the basis of everything you do for your child. Look within yourself. Are you placing your own ambitions on your child's shoulders because you see that as a victory in your own life? Are you aiming to raise a super successful child for your own validation? Be honest. Are you manipulating your child's mind to be dependent on you because you see them as your only support in old age?

3. Instilling moral values in your child

Raising a morally correct child who knows the difference between right and wrong starts with you. Teach them about choices. In every situation, there will always be a choice: the choice to do the right thing as opposed to the easy thing.

4. Embracing parental responsibility

We don't need to be our child's friends because they have many of those. We need to be the parents because as a mother or fathers, we might be all they have. Many times, when we scold our children or make decisions they are unhappy with, it is scary to think they may not like us anymore. Parenting is about making tough calls and not being afraid to be disliked or even hated at the moment.

Parenting in today's time is a constant struggle—a battle against outside distractions and the peer pressure our children may feel. It can sometimes feel overwhelming. As parents, we can only try our best. Here are a few strategies that I, as a parent, always try to implement, which may be helpful for others too.

I try to tell my children every day how much I love them. I tell them that no matter what situation they are in, even if they have made a mistake, they must come back to me. Even if the whole world is against them, I will stand behind them and support them always. My love is unconditional; it does not depend on their school, college ranking or their job. I love them simply because they are my child and nothing can change that.

Apart from close blood relationships, several others come into our lives by choice. These could be friends, colleagues or acquaintances we meet daily or occasionally. It's up to you how much you want to invest in these relationships. Setting clear boundaries in each will help avoid unnecessary heartache.

Consider your expectations from a senior at work or a colleague. Are you looking for more understanding from them than they are willing to give? This mismatch can lead to distress. Often, we mistake a working relationship for friendship simply because we spend a lot of time together during working hours, team dinners, or annual functions. In reality, it may dissolve the day one of you quits.

Identifying your position in someone else's life, whether at work or in general, is crucial for setting clear expectations. This requires self-awareness. How aware are you of yourself and others?

Do you accept everything that has happened in your life up till now, or are you constantly burdened by regret? This self-awareness will significantly influence your life.

People with personalities that constantly dwell on past events with regret often blame those events for their current limitations. The key is to recognize oneself.

'What are your strengths and weaknesses?' This is a common question asked in HR interviews but answering it honestly can benefit us in many ways.

Of all the relationships we've discussed, the most crucial one is with ourselves. We judge and talk to ourselves constantly on a daily basis.

There are times when I don't need anyone to torment or make me unhappy. I can do it all by myself. I'm sure you all realise this is true. We can be our own worst enemies.

That's why it's crucial to recognize what kind of person you are. Before understanding the outside world, know yourself.

Here are a few questions to help you get started.

1. What would you say is your basic nature? Do you call yourself an introvert, an extrovert or a shy person? Are these your own conclusions or a narrative set by your family and friends that you have come to believe over time?

2. Do you understand your reactions on a day-

to-day basis? Can you predict how you will react in a particular situation or is it always a reaction from your side based on the event that is taking place?

3. Are you happy with yourself? This will include your physical as well as your mental makeup. Do you constantly criticise yourself in the mirror or only see your shortcomings?

4. Are you happy in the basic relationships of your life with your parents, siblings, spouse and children?

5. Are you able to autocorrect? Realise where you are wrong and what can be done to make things better.

By adulthood, we may not have all the answers, but we should have learned some things about ourselves. Major life events such as marriage, the death of a loved one, or childbirth can reveal insights into our character. Reflecting on how we acted in these situations, how we handled them and whether we're satisfied with our behaviour can provide valuable self-understanding. Studying ourselves and seeking answers to our questions is essential. Only when we truly understand ourselves can we effectively manage our personality, emotions and relationships.

CHAPTER 6

The Personality Tests

One way of studying one's own and other's personality can be with the help of personality tests. These are used and may help in getting a better understanding of our own self and also other individuals. A number of workplaces now routinely screen potential new candidates with personality tests to have a better understanding of where they might fit into the organisation. Forbes has listed the top 5 best personality tests of 2024 as:

1. Myers-Briggs Type Indicator

2. Big Five

3. CliftonStrengths

4. DISC Profile

5. Enneagram

Myers-Briggs Type Indicator

The Myers-Briggs Type Indicator (MBTI) is a psychological assessment tool designed to measure personality preferences and how people perceive the world and make decisions. It was developed by Isabel Briggs Myers and her mother, Katharine Cook Briggs, based on Carl Jung's theory of psychological types. The MBTI categories individuals into one of sixteen personality types based on four dichotomies:

1. Extraversion (E) vs. Introversion (I):

Extraversion: Preference for drawing energy from the external world of people and activities.

Introversion: Preference for drawing energy from the internal world of thoughts and reflections.

2. Sensing (S) vs. Intuition (N):

Sensing: Preference for focusing on concrete information gained from the five senses.

Intuition: Preference for focusing on abstract information and patterns and the possibilities of what could be.

3. Thinking (T) vs. Feeling (F):

Thinking: Preference for making decisions based on objective logic and analysis.

Feeling: Preference for making decisions based on personal values and the impact on others.

4. Judging (J) vs. Perceiving (P):

Judging: Preference for a structured and organised lifestyle with planned activities.

Perceiving: Preference for a flexible and spontaneous lifestyle, keeping options open.

Each individual's type is represented by a combination of one letter from each dichotomy, resulting in sixteen possible personality types (e.g.,

INTJ, ESFP). The MBTI is widely used in personal development, career counselling, team building and relationship counselling. It helps individuals understand their own personality traits, strengths and potential areas for growth, as well as improve their interactions with others.

Big Five

The Big Five personality test, also known as the Five Factor Model (FFM), is a widely recognized framework for understanding personality traits. It assesses individuals based on five broad dimensions of personality, which are:

1. Openness to Experience (O):

High Score: Imaginative, curious, open-minded and willing to explore new ideas and experiences.

Low Score: Practical, conventional and preferring routine and familiarity.

2. Conscientiousness (C):

High Score: Organized, disciplined, reliable and goal-oriented.

Low Score: Spontaneous, careless and less focused on detail and planning.

3. Extraversion (E):

High Score: Sociable, outgoing, energetic and assertive.

Low Score: Reserved, quiet and more comfortable being alone or in small groups.

4. Agreeableness (A):

High Score: Compassionate, cooperative, trusting and good-natured.

Low Score: Competitive, critical, uncooperative and sometimes antagonistic.

5. Neuroticism (N):

High Score: Anxious, moody, sensitive and prone to experiencing negative emotions.

Low Score: Emotionally stable, calm and less prone to stress.

Each dimension represents a spectrum, with individuals falling somewhere along the continuum for each trait. The Big Five model is based on extensive empirical research and is considered a reliable and valid measure of personality. It is used in various fields, including psychology, human resources and personal development, to understand personality traits and predict behaviour and preferences.

CliftonStrengths

The Clifton Strengths assessment, formerly known as the StrengthsFinder, is a psychological tool developed by the Gallup Organization to identify an individual's unique combination of strengths. The assessment is based on the idea that focusing on strengths rather than weaknesses can lead to greater personal and professional success. The test identifies thirty-four distinct strengths or 'talent themes,' which are grouped into four broad categories:

1. Executing

Themes in this category: Achiever, Arranger, Belief, Consistency, Deliberative, Discipline, Focus, Responsibility, Restorative.

Characteristics: Individuals strong in executing are adept at turning ideas into reality and making things happen. They are dependable, reliable and hardworking.

2. Influencing

Themes in this category: Activator, Command, Communication, Competition, Maximizer, Self-Assurance, Significance, Woo (Winning Others Over).

Characteristics: Individuals strong in influencing excel at persuading others, taking charge and making their presence felt. They are skilled at selling ideas and influencing opinions.

3. Relationship Building

Themes in this category: Adaptability, Connectedness, Developer, Empathy, Harmony, Includer, Individualization, Positivity, Relator.

Characteristics: Individuals strong in relationship building are adept at forming strong bonds, creating cohesive teams and fostering a positive environment. They are empathetic, supportive and great at collaboration.

4. Strategic Thinking

Themes in this category: Analytical, Context,

Futuristic, Ideation, Input, Intellection, Learner, Strategic.

Characteristics: Individuals strong in strategic thinking excel at analysing information, thinking ahead, generating ideas and understanding complex concepts. They are insightful, curious and focused on the future.

The Clifton Strengths assessment provides individuals with a detailed report highlighting their top strengths and offering insights on how to leverage them effectively in various aspects of their lives. It is widely used in personal development, career coaching, leadership training and team building to help individuals and organisations maximise their potential by focusing on their natural talents.

DISC Profile

The DISC Profile test is a behavioural assessment tool based on the DISC theory, originally developed by psychologist William Marston. It categorises behaviour into four main personality traits: Dominance, Influence, Steadiness and Conscientiousness. The DISC Profile helps individuals understand their behaviour, communication style and interaction preferences. Here's a brief overview of each trait:

1. Dominance (D)

Characteristics: Assertive, results-oriented, strong-willed and direct. Individuals high in Dominance are driven by challenge and control, preferring to take charge and make quick decisions.

Focus: Accomplishing tasks, achieving goals and overcoming obstacles.

2. Influence (I)

Characteristics: Sociable, enthusiastic, persuasive and talkative. Individuals high in Influence are motivated by social recognition and interactions, enjoying collaboration and influencing others.

Focus: Building relationships, motivating others and creating a positive environment.

3. Steadiness (S)

Characteristics: Calm, dependable, patient and supportive. Individuals high in Steadiness value consistency and harmony, preferring stable environments and reliable routines.

Focus: Providing support, maintaining stability and ensuring collaboration.

4. Conscientiousness (C)

Characteristics: Analytical, detail-oriented, systematic and precise. Individuals high in Conscientiousness are driven by accuracy and quality, valuing structure and careful planning.

Focus: Ensuring accuracy, maintaining standards and focusing on details.

The DISC Profile test involves a series of questions designed to evaluate an individual's tendencies across these four dimensions. The results provide a detailed report that helps individuals understand their dominant traits and how they influence their behaviour and interactions with others. The DISC model is widely used in personal development, team building, leadership training and organisational development to improve communication, enhance teamwork and optimise individual and group performance.

Enneagram

The Enneagram test is a personality assessment tool that identifies nine distinct personality types, each with its own unique set of motivations, fears and behaviour patterns. The Enneagram model helps individuals understand their core personality, the underlying drivers of their behaviour and pathways for personal growth. Here's a brief overview of the nine Enneagram types:

1. Type 1: The Reformer (The Perfectionist)

Characteristics: Principled, purposeful, self-controlled and perfectionistic.

Core Motivation: Striving for moral integrity and correctness.

Basic Fear: Being corrupt or defective.

2. Type 2: The Helper (The Giver)

Characteristics: Caring, empathetic, generous and people-pleasing.

Core Motivation: Feeling loved and needed by others.

Basic Fear: Being unwanted or unloved.

3. Type 3: The Achiever (The Performer)

Characteristics: Ambitious, adaptable, image-conscious and success-oriented.

Core Motivation: Being admired and successful.

Basic Fear: Being worthless or a failure.

4. Type 4: The Individualist (The Romantic)

Characteristics: Creative, sensitive, introspective and expressive.

Core Motivation: Finding and expressing their unique identity.

Basic Fear: Having no identity or personal significance.

5. Type 5: The Investigator (The Thinker)

Characteristics: Analytical, perceptive, innovative and detached.

Core Motivation: Understanding the world and being competent.

Basic Fear: Being helpless or incapable.

6. Type 6: The Loyalist (The Skeptic)

Characteristics: Loyal, responsible, anxious and security-oriented.

Core Motivation: Seeking safety and support.

Basic Fear: Being without support or guidance.

7. Type 7: The Enthusiast (The Epicure)

Characteristics: Enthusiastic, spontaneous, fun-loving and adventurous.

Core Motivation: Seeking happiness and avoiding pain.

Basic Fear: Being deprived or in pain.

8. Type 8: The Challenger (The Protector)

Characteristics: Assertive, strong, decisive and protective.

Core Motivation: Asserting control and protecting themselves.

Basic Fear: Being harmed or controlled by others.

9. Type 9: The Peacemaker (The Mediator)

Characteristics: Easygoing, agreeable, complacent and conflict-averse.

Core Motivation:** Maintaining inner peace and harmony.

Basic Fear: Loss and separation.

The Enneagram test involves a series of questions that assess an individual's tendencies and preferences, leading to the identification of their dominant type. Each type also has connections to other types, called 'wings' (adjacent types) and 'lines' (directions of integration and disintegration), which add depth to the understanding of an individual's personality. The Enneagram is widely used for personal development, relationship counselling, team building and spiritual growth.

All the personality tests in the world will not help us if we do not understand and accept who we are. As children grow up, we gradually learn about the people at home, then our friends and maybe gradually come to an understanding of ourselves. A lot of people never make the effort to learn, unlearn or become better. They are happy in their lives. The awakened ones will try to understand the world. And ourselves in it.

What is the purpose of your life?

If you have never asked this question yourself, maybe now is a good time to do so.

All of us need not be world-changing leaders, we can be happy in our own simple life that is good enough.

The purpose of our life is to be happy. To live honestly with ourselves and everyone around us. To not harm. To love and be loved. The purpose of life is to live with pure intent. That is why it is so important to know oneself.

Study your own self. Listen to your thoughts. Analyse what you are thinking.

We take care of our body so well, we dress it up, exercise it, feed it. In contrast, we constantly abuse and misuse our minds. We feed it junk on social media, we lie, manipulate and think of ourselves as being very smart.

The mind is a very powerful instrument. It is also like a monkey dancing from one thought to another. Are you able to control your mind or does it run here and there at the smallest provocation? Can anyone or anything set the monkey to dance or are you able to sit it down quietly in a place and assess what needs to be done?

What are you doing when you are alone?

If no one is watching will you still always do the correct thing?

This is your moral compass. A person who is true to self will treat himself with respect too. It does not matter what others think of me but it matters what I think of myself. If you do not respect yourself, how do you expect others to do the same for you?

We always know in our hearts what we have done wrong. In the end, this should matter.

One way of trying to assess this self-awareness is to study our own Emotional Intelligence. Learning about our emotional intelligence helps one to assess oneself and others a little better.

So, what is this emotional intelligence?

CHAPTER 7

Emotional Intelligence

Emotional Intelligence is the ability to perceive, use, understand, manage and handle emotions. Simply put, it involves recognizing your feelings in a given situation and responding appropriately. It also entails being aware of and sensitive to others' emotions and situations and reacting suitably.

Why do we consider emotional intelligence so important? This is because most of our daily lives involve interactions with others and managing situations at work or home. Understanding others better helps avoid many potential negative impacts, both short-term and long-term.

In our day-to-day life, we meet many people. Understanding the type of person we are dealing with and our reactions to them helps us avoid unnecessary confrontations and heartache. Being emotionally aware also includes anticipating situations, which allows us to control many variables in our lives. While we can't control everything due to life's inherent unpredictability, we can train ourselves to handle difficult or unpredictable situations better.

I'll share a small example. Whenever we have to travel, I get stressed out about multiple things, which often leads to me yelling and getting angry with my kids before we leave the house. This has happened many times and now I realise that I tend to lose my cool because of the stress involved. Although I still feel stressed, I try to avoid aggravating the children by screaming at them, which only leads to bad moods and unnecessary unhappiness. Instead, I let them know that I'm feeling stressed and ask for their help. While kids don't always listen and we still have occasional meltdowns, the intensity and aftereffects are now a bit better. The kids even call this 'the monster mom' who comes out whenever I'm stressed. I also tend to feel very low whenever they get sick and often end up scolding the sick child, which is another avoidable situation. I need to understand what I'm feeling and why, without letting it overwhelm me.

Although we develop a certain level of emotional intelligence based on the environment we are raised in, many of us need to hone these skills further. This is particularly relevant in today's times. With smaller, nuclear families becoming the norm, our day-to-day interactions with other people have decreased. The households with only one or two children face unique challenges.

In such families, the child often becomes the centre of attention, with everything revolving around them. I've observed parents who fear their child's reactions which has made the child more fragile. They struggle to handle small stressors and even a comment on social media can trigger significant emotional reactions. Just imagine – a comment from an unknown person, someone you've never met or seen, has the power to make you happy or deeply unhappy.

This is why emotional intelligence plays an important role in our lives. It helps us manage our own emotions as well as those of others. It aids in understanding stress and handling it better. An emotionally stable person will have more stable relationships and won't be easily broken when a relationship doesn't work out. Just as emotional intelligence can be improved upon, it can also be tested. Studies on emotional intelligence have been ongoing since the 1960s when Daniel Goleman first introduced the term.

Emotional intelligence can be assessed in various ways but two common methods are self-report assessments and performance-based tests. Here's a brief overview of each:

1. Self-Report Assessments

These tests involve individuals rating their own emotional skills and behaviours. They typically consist of questionnaires or surveys where participants respond to statements about their emotional abilities, such as empathy, emotional regulation and interpersonal skills.

Example:

- Emotional Quotient Inventory (EQ-i): Developed by Reuven Bar-On, this test measures various aspects of emotional and social functioning, such as self-perception, stress management and relationship skills.

- ⊙ Schutte Self-Report Emotional Intelligence Test (SSEIT): This test assesses four dimensions of emotional intelligence: perception of emotion, managing own emotions, managing others' emotions and utilisation of emotions.

2. Performance-Based Tests

These tests involve individuals completing tasks or solving problems that require emotional skills. They are designed to measure actual abilities rather than self-perceived skills. These tests often assess how well individuals can identify, understand and manage emotions in themselves and others.

Example:

- ⊙ Mayer-Salovey-Caruso Emotional Intelligence Test (MSCEIT): Developed by John Mayer, Peter Salovey and David Caruso, this test measures four branches of emotional intelligence: perceiving emotions, using emotions to facilitate thought, understanding emotions and managing emotions. It includes tasks like identifying emotions in faces, generating emotions to solve problems and understanding emotional changes.

Both methods have their strengths and limitations. Self-report assessments are relatively easy to administer and provide insight into how individuals view their own emotional abilities. However, they can be influenced by social desirability bias and may not accurately reflect actual skills. Performance-based tests offer a more objective measure of emotional abilities but can be more complex and time-consuming to administer. Combining both methods can provide a more comprehensive assessment of an individual's emotional intelligence.

Emotional Intelligence is not a vague concept. It is made up of 4 components. These are mainly:

1. Self-awareness

2. Self-regulation

3. Social awareness

4. Relationship management

Let's look at each of these concepts in detail.

Self-awareness

This is self-explanatory. How well do I know myself? How aware am I of my own feelings? How well do I understand my behaviour in different settings? In our day-to-day lives, each of us plays many roles. We are truly actors. We may present ourselves differently in front of our boss, colleagues and juniors. At home, our parents see us in a different light compared to how our spouses or children see us.

An emotionally sound person can easily understand the requirements of different roles and switch between them with ease. You cannot bring your morning fight with your spouse to the office and scold your juniors because of it. This behaviour is unprofessional and must be avoided.

Recognizing our own emotions and their impact on those around us is crucial. Only small children have the luxury of expressing every emotion they feel. If a baby is uncomfortable, they cry; if they are rested and happy, they play. This is a beautiful, carefree time. However, as we grow older, we need to understand the power of our emotions and learn to manage them effectively.

Well-handled emotions can take us to great heights, but emotions not managed appropriately can damage our relationships both at home and in the workplace.

Self-awareness can be taught to children starting at a young age. We can have conversations about how the child felt in particular situations. For example, we can ask how they feel before a class test. Are they nervous? A child who recognizes that it is normal to feel these emotions may be able to handle them better. Instead of saying, 'Don't be scared, your exam will go well,' we can say, 'It's okay to feel scared. Take a deep breath, say a little prayer and drink some water before the exam.' This approach conveys that these emotions are part of the process and can be managed. Similarly, sharing that it's okay to be anxious before receiving test results will help them express what they feel.

Self Regulation

Recognizing your emotions, managing them

and understanding where to express them is self-regulation.

No matter how angry she is, a mother knows she cannot scream at her child in front of others at a party. That will have to wait until they reach home. This is a basic and simple example that many of us have experienced as children and as parents.

On a day-to-day basis, we go through various emotions and moods. The two are not the same.

Emotions are clear feelings that arise from a specific event and are short-term. For example, if I go to pick up my dress from the tailor and it is not ready, I get angry and upset.

Moods, on the other hand, are vaguer and may occur without a particular trigger, lasting for a longer duration. For example, I might feel low and upset when I wake up, even though my life is exactly the same as it was yesterday. This is a mood.

Emotions can be positive or negative in how they make us feel. Happiness, sadness, fear, disgust, anger, surprise, shame and pride are all classified as emotions. Moods can also be positive or negative and can be described in many ways, such as excited, cheerful, motivated, enthusiastic, low, upset and unhappy.

A key element in differentiating between these two is their duration. Emotions may come and go quickly, while moods tend to last longer.

I received a bunch of flowers unexpectedly and

I felt happy and cheerful. Similarly, if I get angry with a child at home in the morning but then calm down as I leave for work, this is self-regulation.

Many people I know tend to amplify their emotions in their minds, allowing them to influence their mood for an entire day or even longer. This often hinges on how they speak to themselves.

We all have an inner dialogue every day and the most constant voice in our heads is our own. The way we talk to ourselves is crucial because it significantly impacts our lives. Our minds listen to what we say, shaping our thoughts and actions accordingly. If we affirm, 'I am strong and capable,' we are more likely to find ways to achieve our goals. Conversely, if we say, 'This will never happen,' we may inadvertently hinder ourselves. The power of the mind is profound, as evidenced by countless books on the subject. Therefore, it's essential to be mindful of our self-talk and its implications.

Most people can be broadly categorised into two personality types: positive and negative.

Positive individuals are generally cheerful in their day-to-day lives. They speak with enthusiasm, encourage themselves and others and focus on highlighting good qualities. During conflicts, they actively seek solutions and ask, 'How can this be resolved?'

The greatest quality of positive people is their recognition of the transient nature of all events, especially adversity.

'This too shall pass.' This isn't just a statement; it's a fundamental truth of life. Positive individuals understand that even when they remain inactive, life continues around them. They grasp the idea that current situations are temporary and believe in eventual improvement. Their optimistic outlook extends to people and life in general, enabling them to navigate hardships more effectively.

Negative people, on the other hand, tend to focus on what is wrong in a situation. They seek out aspects they dislike in people or situations and fixate on these issues.

They often feel apprehensive and avoid taking risks. Negative individuals can be excessively self-conscious and may struggle with low self-esteem. When presented with a new event or proposal, their initial reaction tends to be 'no.' They are adept at finding reasons why something cannot be accomplished.

Personality traits are up to a certain extent set in us as we grow older. We can train ourselves to handle our situations better. A few key steps to self-regulate can be:

1. Preparing for Emotional Challenges

I know I don't like someone and I will meet this person at this event, so I can mentally prepare to feel a bit upset. However, I am aware of this beforehand and I believe I can handle it.

2. Self-Reflection and Emotional Awareness

What am I telling myself all the time or in this

particular situation? Recognizing the emotion I am feeling right now. Accepting it.

3. Choosing Fight or Flight: Assessing the Situation

Whether this is a situation that needs me to fight or flight?

It is crucial to remain aware of our state of mind at all times. I control my mind, not the other way around. Throughout the day, many emotions arise within us, but we have the ability to choose which ones to act upon and which to disregard. Unlike babies, who can go with the flow, the rest of us must adapt to our emotions consciously.

Moods, on the other hand, are a bit more challenging to handle. Because they lack a clear-cut reason or trigger, it can be difficult to alleviate them. Sometimes, we can simply allow them to exist, continue with our daily activities and wait for them to subside. However, if a negative mood persists for an extended period, it may be necessary to seek external support. This could involve reaching out to your family or consulting with a professional.

Moods can also be influenced by our internal environment, with hormones playing a significant role in altering them. While not all moods can be attributed to hormonal factors, some can.

For instance, if a hormonal imbalance is causing frequent and severe mood swings, it is important to investigate and seek appropriate treatment.

Hormones are chemical substances that act as messenger molecules in the body. They are produced in one part of the body and travel to and affect other organs. Human beings have numerous hormones, some of which are well-known. For example, insulin, produced in the pancreas, regulates sugar levels in our body. The thyroid gland secretes thyroid hormone and testosterone is responsible for masculine features in males. Females produce progesterone and oestrogen, known as female hormones. Oxytocin, often called the bonding hormone, also plays a crucial role in social bonding and childbirth.

An imbalance in hormones can lead to mood swings. For instance, abnormal thyroid levels—whether too low or too high—can cause irritability, anxiety and lethargy. Hormones play an especially significant role during adolescence and menopause, often causing turmoil and unexplained emotions. Support and understanding from family members can be invaluable during these critical periods.

We often hear about 'feel-good' hormones like dopamine, serotonin and endorphins. These neurotransmitters in our brains help regulate happiness. Engaging in activities such as exercise or pursuing hobbies we enjoy can elevate the levels of these hormones in our bodies, contributing to a positive mood.

We must recognize what we are experiencing and why. This self-awareness is essential for monitoring our emotions and thoughts, which is the first step toward self-healing. Self-healing or self-soothing is vital for our well-being. If you rely on others to make you happy, there's an imbalance in that equation.

Happiness is an inside job. Each person should take responsibility for their own mental well-being. Regardless of your circumstances or relationships, if you cannot manage your reactions and emotions, you may struggle to find happiness. It's okay to experience all emotions—I can acknowledge my anger at someone who has betrayed me and my sadness about the situation—but it's crucial to understand what I'm going through and why.

This self-awareness helps in controlling reactions and recovering more quickly. Learning to control your mind and gain perspective can be a significant victory in itself.

Social Awareness

Social Awareness involves recognizing and understanding others' feelings. Empathy, closely linked to social awareness, means putting ourselves in another person's shoes and experiencing what they are feeling in that moment. One of the simplest ways to enhance social awareness is to improve our listening and observation skills. Giving others the opportunity to share their perspectives before jumping to conclusions not only enhances understanding but also allows us to respond thoughtfully, particularly in emotionally charged situations.

Social awareness is particularly crucial in workplace environments where you interact with diverse individuals in various circumstances. While you may not always have the time to know everyone's full background, a perceptive leader or team player can discern situations effectively.

For instance, if a long-time employee starts arriving late daily, it may turn out that she recently got married and her new home is further away. A conversation reveals she's searching for a closer residence, but the move will take time. A good leader understands this situation as temporary and values the employee's contribution enough not to jeopardise it over such a matter.

A less effective leader with inadequate skills might call the employee into their office frequently to lecture them on how their tardiness affects work. This approach could lead to the employee resigning, resulting in the loss of a valuable team member. It also reflects poorly on the leader's ability to assess situations and consider both short-term and long-term implications.

While everyone is replaceable to some extent, a competent leader recognizes the value of skilled team members. This underscores the critical importance of having leaders in key positions who possess strong social awareness.

Relationship Management

Relationships are inevitable in our lives, ranging from lifelong bonds with our parents to fleeting connections with daily acquaintances. While some relationships are beyond our control, many are chosen and nurtured over time.

Those with strong relationship skills can adapt to various relationship dynamics according to their needs. Understanding the intentions others have toward us is crucial for leading a fulfilling life.

Every human being, in every situation, including ourselves, has an intention. For example, a mother's intention towards her baby is typically pure, focused on keeping the child safe, secure and cared for to the best of her ability.

Understanding and interpreting another person's intentions takes time and often comes with experience and maturity.

Most people tend to see in others a reflection of their own selves. A person with a straightforward and honest approach to life may naturally assume that others are similarly honest and trustworthy until they learn otherwise through experience. Conversely, a manipulative individual may perceive others as cunning as well. This dynamic often forms the foundation of many relationships.

For example, a dishonest person may struggle with trust issues and harbour suspicions in their interactions. In contrast, an honest person strives to maintain clarity and transparency in all relationships, even though they may sometimes face negative consequences due to the nature of the other person involved.

There are many instances where we may not approve of a child's friend because we can perceive something about them that our child cannot yet see.

This perception is shaped by our past experiences and understanding of the other person's intentions.

Teaching our children this life skill is crucial. Not everyone they encounter deserves their time and trust. We must guide them to observe nonverbal cues, develop intuition and not always take spoken words at face value, but instead, assess the actions behind those words. Sadly, in today's world, it's a reality that few people can be fully trusted. Many individuals may have hidden agendas or intentions that do not align with how they present themselves to us.

CHAPTER 8

Relationships and Society

Society is defined as the aggregate of people living together in a more or less ordered community. Human societies are structured around relationships, labour and societal roles. Human behaviour is categorised based on clearly defined roles and actions are judged as either good or bad according to established norms. For instance, stealing is universally considered bad behaviour and can be punished according to societal rules.

As individuals, we have an innate desire to belong and be accepted within our community. It matters to us what others think of us and we strive to understand and fulfil our designated roles as best as we can. Deviating from these roles often involves significant challenges and conflicts.

Humans are inherently social beings who seek acceptance and approval, often conforming to societal norms and expectations.

In earlier times, roles were more defined: fathers were providers, mothers were nurturers. However, over time, these roles have become less clear, leading to internal and societal conflicts. For example, a father may resist his role as a provider and shirk responsibilities, while a mother may find herself as a single parent fulfilling multiple roles in the household. Similarly, a young woman aspiring to work abroad may be pressured into marriage and homemaking, causing resentment and unhappiness.

In the past, people tended to accept their assigned roles to a certain extent. However, with the influence of social media and television, aspirations and expectations have expanded, leading to greater aspirations and sometimes dissatisfaction with traditional roles.

We are constantly comparing ourselves to others and often feel inadequate as a result. It seems like nothing is ever enough because there's always something bigger and better out there that we feel compelled to achieve. As a society, we've lost sight of the importance of being content with where we are, instead of constantly chasing after new goals. This pressure is often amplified by the constant stream of social media posts that bombard us.

Society, at its core, is composed of individuals, so any meaningful change must begin with each person. To understand the larger patterns at play, we must study individual behaviours across various situations. The uniqueness of each human lies in their individuality—every person holds their own distinct ideas, thoughts, beliefs and behaviours.

This unpredictability can be confusing, leading us to seek patterns in behaviour to better anticipate how individuals will react in various situations. For instance, when I find myself in a room with another person, I typically initiate a conversation unless there are explicit rules against it, or circumstances prevent either of us from doing so.

The basic human tendency is to conform to societal norms because we seek acceptance and affection from those around us. Occasionally, we encounter people or news that shocks us, prompting us to question how someone could behave in such ways.

This could involve acts of extraordinary courage, such as risking one's life to save another or renouncing worldly possessions to pursue a spiritual life. Conversely, shocking news continues to escalate in horror, such as incidents like child rape, murder, or brutal acts like setting someone on fire.

What does this tell us? That humans are capable of a wide range of behaviours. A person's behaviour is influenced by various factors: their inherent nature, personality, education, upbringing, circumstances and sometimes, provocation. Interestingly, people may behave differently in groups than they would individually. This phenomenon is often referred to as Mob Mentality.

Mob Mentality is commonly observed in riots and wars, where individuals may set aside their own feelings and get swept up in the prevailing emotions of the group. This behaviour can be driven by fear as well—the fear of standing out or being perceived differently from everyone else in the group.

Human behaviour on an individual level can be categorised in various ways. For instance, behaviour can be classified as voluntary or involuntary, where overt behaviour is observable, contrasting with covert behaviour that encompasses internal mental processes. Additionally, social behaviour involves interactions with others, which are extensively studied in psychology.

From a broader perspective, common classifications of behaviour can be simplified into four categories:

1. Optimistic

2. Pessimistic

3. Trusting

4. Envious

Although it is tempting to categorise people into simple classifications, in reality, human beings are far from unidimensional. They are complex and multifaceted. It's common to live with a spouse for many years and still be taken aback by sudden changes in behaviour. This variability occurs because human behaviour itself is subject to change over time.

Some of the common traits seen in the different types of people are:

Optimistic Traits

Optimistic people maintain a positive attitude towards life. When faced with setbacks or failures, they might feel down temporarily but quickly bounce back. They are generally cheerful and happier in their daily lives. Expecting good things to happen, they express gratitude when they do. Optimistic individuals are more likely to achieve success because they take more risks, driven by a strong sense of self-confidence. Their positivity also makes them enjoyable to be around, as they uplift and inspire those around them.

A significant downside of optimism is that overly optimistic people can often have their heads in the clouds, lacking a realistic or practical approach to reality. They always assume that good things will happen, leaving them unprepared when they don't. This sudden shift can cause anxiety, which they may struggle to handle. Their false sense of security leads them to believe that things will work out, so they often fail to plan for adverse events. Consequently, their future planning may not be practical for day-to-day life. While optimism is a good personality trait, optimistic individuals benefit from having realistic partners who can provide a necessary reality check from time to time.

Pessimistic Traits

Pessimism is a personality trait often associated with negative thinking. Pessimistic individuals are typically more practical and realistic in their outlook on life. While often seen as a negative trait, it has its merits. Pessimistic people are grounded in reality and adept at identifying potential pitfalls. However, problems arise when they focus exclusively on what can go wrong, neglecting the potential for positive outcomes. They are low-risk takers and resistant to change, often remaining disturbed for extended periods until they adapt to new circumstances. Despite their ability to anticipate problems, pessimistic people struggle to handle stress when things go wrong. They are more prone to depression and anxiety disorders and can often bring apprehension into family dynamics.

Trusting Personality Traits

Many times, we encounter people who are childlike in their beliefs and take things at face value. These individuals, characterised by gullibility and naivety, exhibit trusting personality traits. Often having a positive attitude towards life, they generally lead happier lives because they see the good in everyone. They are trustworthy themselves and follow through on their word, often believing others will do the same. They are the first to help others and are frequently taken advantage of, but they rarely learn to be cautious. With age, some of these individuals learn to differentiate between genuine and deceitful intentions. Parents often worry about how the world will treat a child with a trusting personality, fearing they may be easily misled. Pure-hearted, generous and simple are often adjectives used to describe such people.

Envious Personalities

An envious person is self-centred and rarely feels happy for someone else's success. They don't want others to achieve anything and are jealous of anything good happening to them. With age, envious people often learn to mask their true nature, displaying fake emotions when faced with someone else's success, but they cannot maintain this facade for long. At a success party or celebration, they might smile and hide their true feelings, but their nonverbal cues often give them away. They love to gossip and take pleasure in another person's misfortune, which they then share with others. Few people will admit to this side of themselves, openly confessing that they didn't feel happy about someone else's good news. We lie to others, but we also lie to ourselves a lot. Fake people are never true to themselves either; they present a different version of themselves than who they really are and will have an excuse for everything they do.

As human beings, we are not unidimensional; we have many layers. How we see ourselves and how others see us may be entirely different, but who are we to judge anyone?

CHAPTER 9

Recognising Behaviours

Life is not black and white; it is grey. What may be right for me may seem wrong for you. I might see a person as being optimistic, while you might see the same person as a dreamer with unrealistic ambitions, always chasing unachievable goals with their head in the clouds. A childlike person in today's world might be an easy target for manipulation and scheming, raising the question of whether this is a good personality to have or a poor one. Pessimistic or negative people may be high achievers because they think practically and do not harbour false hopes about situations.

Manipulative people are often people pleasers who know how to get their work done, which may be considered a good quality in today's world. In short, there is no good or bad; there are just different types of people we will meet in our lives or different facets of the same person. A significant step in self-growth is recognizing the various aspects of a person and learning how to coexist with them. We ourselves may have many layers and, often, we do not recognize the toxic behaviours we are capable of. The most common behaviours can be found all around us and within ourselves.

Let's look at some of the examples.

1. The People Pleasers

These are the people who are always seeking to look good in others' eyes, craving constant external validation to affirm they are good people. Such individuals often harbour an inferiority complex or feel unloved. They may have had an unhappy childhood or been overshadowed by siblings, finding that the only way to achieve recognition was by pleasing someone and getting into their good books.

2. The Huge Egos

In gatherings, we often encounter people who observe but never initiate a greeting or smile. These individuals exhibit egotistical personality traits, often viewing themselves highly and holding a superiority complex. Typically, they may possess special attributes such as financial wealth, higher education, old-school values, or a royal background. They look down on others and consider themselves superior to those around them. They tend to be critical of everything and often lead unhappy day-to-day lives because they are easily displeased.

3. The Dishwasher

I refer to people who consistently dampen your spirits as 'dishwashers.' Whatever you share with them, they find a way to cast a shadow over it, leaving you feeling disheartened after every interaction. Often driven by envy and jealousy, they derive satisfaction from belittling others. Upon closer interaction, you'll notice that these individuals are typically negative thinkers, insecure about their own abilities and project these feelings onto their conversations.

4. Divide and Rule

Often, both at home and in the workplace, some individuals always strive to be the go-to person for others. They crave attention and dislike it when others form bonds without them. They may engage in gossip or subtle deception to create discord between others while maintaining their own connections. Highly cunning and manipulative, they adeptly seize opportunities to benefit themselves from every situation.

5. The Lost Person

In today's world, what I might call a trusting personality could be seen as naive. They often lack awareness of what's happening around them, which can lead them to be taken advantage of or make them appear foolish. While they may learn with time, their basic nature remains straightforward. They react to situations without much consideration of ulterior motives. Over time, they need to gain a deeper understanding of how the world operates.

6. The Victim

They often revel in feeling sad and depressed about themselves. Phrases like 'Nothing ever goes in my favour' or 'Why do things never work out for me?' are their favourites. These individuals tend to make everything about themselves. For instance, if a victim's personality is caring for a sick person, soon enough you'll hear how challenging it has been for them to look after the sick individual. Consequently, the attention shifts from the sick person to the victim, as they always manage to make it about themselves.

7. The Power Trippers

Often found in positions of authority, whether as heads of families or in institutions, these individuals typically exhibit an elevated sense of entitlement. They expect everyone to obey them constantly and require regular displays of respect. Their egos are easily inflated and equally sensitive to the slightest perceived slights. For instance, if someone fails to stand up upon their entry into a room or greets them a bit tardily, they take offence. Subsequently, they demand to be pampered or treated as important to soothe their bruised egos.

8. Self-centred and Self-obsessed

In today's world, this type of person is increasingly common. They show little concern for others' feelings and emotions, with 'I' being the most important word in their vocabulary. Filled with self-importance, they obsess over their own work, clothes, happiness and problems. Those around them often find themselves making significant adjustments and pandering to these individuals to maintain peace. Having a self-obsessed spouse or child can profoundly impact others involved, as their feelings are rarely considered or valued.

9. The Sacrificial Resentful Person

No matter how many sacrifices we make, it's true that others often forget after some time. Equally true is that saying 'yes' a hundred times and 'no' the 101st time can have greater consequences, undoing all previous 'yes' efforts. This is basic human nature. Often, the person who has made countless sacrifices begins to feel unappreciated and unloved over time, leading to internal resentment. Eventually, the giver becomes weary and stops making efforts, burdening the relationship further.

10. Passive Aggressive Behaviour

A person in a household or workplace may refrain from expressing anger due to fear or lack of confidence. This often results in the Silent Treatment, where the person becomes passive-aggressive, neglects tasks, refuses to listen, or pretends not to hear. This behaviour typically continues until the other person is compelled to reconcile with the offended individual. In a parental context, this can be highly distressing. Children, especially when young, depend heavily on their parents, so if a parent uses emotional distance or silent treatment as a form of punishment, it can leave a child feeling insecure and frightened. Such repeated behaviour can leave lasting emotional scars on a child's mental well-being.

11. The Loud Voiced Bully

They are often blessed with a loud, aggressive voice, which they frequently use to assert themselves. Speaking loudly and often disregarding others' opinions, they believe themselves to be right in every situation and tend to overpower those with milder temperaments. While loud-voiced individuals may frequently get their way, they often struggle to maintain successful close relationships because people around them are intimidated by their assertiveness.

12. Emotional Manipulators

These individuals are adept at managing both their own and others' emotions, skillfully using them to achieve their goals. Highly intelligent, they possess sharp instincts and can swiftly assess and adapt to various situations. Often portraying a facade, they are expert manipulators who adjust their behaviour as per the situation's demands. Lacking authenticity, they cannot be relied upon as they change their stance according to convenience. A prominent characteristic is their habitual lying, regardless of the circumstance, as they do not adhere to moral principles and do not consider lying as morally wrong.

CHAPTER 10

Life Lessons I Learnt

We have experienced the various stages of life, encountering different personalities, emotions, moods, and behaviours. We have navigated through society, only to find ourselves returning to our core being.

If you are reading this book, I assume you are an adult seeking a deeper understanding of life, yourself, and the people around you. Life is not the same for everyone. For many, it is easy, but often, it can be extremely challenging and difficult.

An evolved human being is someone who can look around and recognize disparities. Developing empathy, understanding others' pain and struggles, is one of the most admirable qualities you can cultivate. If I recognize the need to help myself or others, I consider myself on the right path.

As individuals, we can develop qualities through consistent effort. Change doesn't happen overnight, but it can happen with perseverance and dedication. By making conscious choices daily, you will notice your personality evolving over time. The person you become may sometimes amaze you. This is the power of transformation. *We all have the ability to transform ourselves into someone better.*

Over the years, I have read many self-help books. It used to be a hobby until I realised that before looking outside, I needed to first look within. Along the way, I've learned a few lessons that I want to share with you all. They might not help everyone, but they may help some of you.

1. Trust yourself

In life, before we can trust anyone else, we must learn to trust ourselves. How do we trust ourselves? By holding ourselves accountable for our words and actions. Respect yourself and build a reputation for keeping your word. Say it aloud to yourself and others: "I do what I say. Always."

Respect yourself and keep your word. If you say something, try your best to do it. If you are unsure about something, don't commit to it. *Words are powerful, so treat them with respect.*

If you sometimes cannot follow through, take the time to explain to the other person why you couldn't. Even if it's something as small as, "I will call you back." If you are not going to call back, don't say it.

2. Learn and upgrade

We are all born with limited skills. Our education, background, and upbringing play significant roles in shaping who we become, but they do not have to define us. Some of the most successful people are those who are willing to reinvent themselves time and again. Life brings new challenges at every stage, so try to do something new to keep yourself and your mind fresh. If you are well off and able to help others, do it.

Most of us will get married, have children, raise them, and retire. We will then spend our years trying to pass the time. But what if you could use these years to make a difference in someone's life? It could be volunteering at a nearby shelter or giving lessons to less privileged children. If you are motivated, you will find a way. If you are not, you will find excuses.

3. Believe in a higher power

Most of us pray, whether to a specific deity or to the universe. Take a few moments each day to connect with the higher power you trust. Make this a part of your routine and set a dedicated time for it. It could be when you wake up, after a bath, or before you go to sleep. Stick to it.

4. Better self awareness and acceptance

No one is perfect, and that's what makes us unique. There are many parts of my own personality that I don't like, but until I undergo a major transformation, I will have to accept myself as I am.

Learning to forgive has been one of the most challenging lessons I've learned over the years—learning to let go of my own mistakes and forgive myself. It's not easy; I often find myself reverting to hurtful and unkind thoughts towards myself. I accept that I am still learning, and this journey may continue until my dying day.

We often judge ourselves based on others'

expectations. Define your own criteria and accept where you are. Life is not a race; it is a journey. Each of us can set our own pace. Do not judge others, and do not allow anyone to judge you.

5. Manifest

All the books written about manifesting what you want cannot fully convey how true this concept is. We have the power to manifest and create the life we desire. It might sound surprisingly simple, but it is indeed true.

My simple plan to manifest:

a. Set a clear, realistic goal in your mind.

b. Identify what you need to make it happen and work towards that.

c. Every day before you sleep, visualise yourself achieving your goal with closed eyes.

d. Keep at it – days, months, years – don't give up. Stay focused and committed to your goal; you will reach it. It might take time, but nothing worthwhile comes easily.

e. Believe, believe, believe.

f. Don't listen to anyone who tells you it won't happen.

6. Live with boundaries and an honest intent

In today's world, this may be challenging but it is essential. At the end of the day, I am accountable to myself and no one else. We all recognize when we've done something wrong; there's no other explanation. We might deceive ourselves with lies and excuses, but deep down, we know the truth.

7. Need less

Learn to be someone who needs less in every aspect of life:

- ⊙ Less money

- ⊙ Less space

- ⊙ Fewer clothes

- ⊙ Less luxury

- ⊙ Less attention

- ⊙ Fewer people

And most importantly, less love. Be sufficient within yourself, for yourself. Spend time discovering your purpose on this earth. Be at peace with yourself and love yourself unconditionally just for being human.

References:

The Oxford Handbook of the history of Psychology. Global Perspectives' Baker D B

Psychology and alchemy C.G. Jung

Self and Identity in modern psychology Paranjpe A.C.

Journal: History of psychology

Child care and the Growth of love,London Penguin books, Bowlby J 1953

Attachment and loss: Bowlby J

Developmental Psychology: Human development across the lifespan

Theories of personality-Understanding persons-Boston-Cloninger S C

Simply psychology-Mc Leod Koreberg

Atul Gawande: Being Mortal

Self-Report measures of depression:Boyle G.J

The science of behaviour: Carlson Neil

Theories and Models of personality: Carthwright, Desmond

Personality types; Jungs model of personality types Pearson education

Emotional Intelligence: Daniel Goleman

Cambridge dictionary: all definitions